Versailles

The King's Pleasure

HUBERT ASTIER

PHOTOGRAPHS
NICOLAS BRUANT

TRANSLATION
MICHAEL TAYLOR

C O N T E N T S

FOREWORD 4

THE GARDEN 7

7 **The King's Pleasure: the Gardens**
- The New Art of Laying Out Gardens
- The Gardens, a Setting for Royal Entertainments

THE CHÂTEAU 33

33 **The King's Glory: the Château**
- Building the Château
- A Symbolic Decoration
- The Hall of Mirrors, a Showcase for the King
- Life at Court

AFTER LOUIS XIV 61

61 **After Louis XIV: New Customs in the Age of Enlightenment**
- Louis XV, the Invention of Private Life
- Louis XVI and Marie-Antoinette

CONCLUSION 78

78 **Versailles yesterday and today**

FOREWORD

As you gaze out at sunset over the Château grounds from the Hall of Mirrors your eye surrenders to their beauty and serenity. Clearly you are in the presence of a dream come true, the dream of a 23-year-old youth, a king of France, enamoured with dancing, beauty and glory.

And yet the site had seemed an unpromising one. This is how Saint Simon, peevish as always, described it a few decades later: "The most cheerless and unprepossessing of all places, lacking a view, lacking woods, lacking water, with no firm land and no air, therefore irremediably insalubrious." Even Colbert, the Superintendent of Public Buildings, pointed out that "nothing distinguishes the greatness and spirit of princes better than buildings; all posterity rates them by the splendid dwellings they erect during their lifetime."

But Colbert was bent on completing what he regarded as the King's grandest undertaking: the Louvre — a project successive French monarchs had been dreaming of for a century. In 1664, the greatest architect of the age was summoned — Bernini, then at the height of his Italian glory. On June 4, 1665, Louis XIV received him at his Château of Saint-Germain. "I do not want to hear any talk of anything small!" exclaimed Il Cavaliere Bernini theatrically. The youthful King replied that he was "in favor of preserving what his predecessors had erected, but that if it was impossible to build something great without tearing down the existing buildings, he was ready to abandon them" to the architect.

And so the project was set in motion and Bernini was not to rebuild the Louvre. "This dwelling is designed for Your Majesty's pleasure and entertainment, not for your glory," objected Colbert. "What a pity if the greatest and most virtuous King were to be measured by the yard-stick of Versailles! And yet there seems to be some reason for fearing such a misfortune."

Why Versailles? What lay behind the young King's obstinacy and crafty manipulation of his entourage, including Colbert who was long led to believe that Louis XIV was mainly interested in expanding the Louvre? Some claim that it was filial love for his father who had been especially fond of his isolated retreat at Versailles. But Louis XIV had not had much contact with his father. Others say that the young King feared Paris, where the Fronde was active. Yet he by no means neglected that city, witness the Invalides and the Place des Victoires, which were built under his reign.

Is not the truth simply that with Versailles, which lay out in the open country, Louis XIV had ample scope to flesh out his dreams of glory, artistic creation and pleasure? Versailles was his greatest accomplishment. Like an alchemist, he turned the lead of an unassuming hunting lodge into the Sun King's gold. Versailles was a pleasure dome, where the youthful King could celebrate each new extension of his gardens with dazzling festivities. He was young, he wanted to enjoy himself and dreamed of being another Alexander the Great — a splendidly attired knight on a high-stepping steed.

Hubert Astier

The King's Pleasure: the Gardens

THE NEW ART OF LAYING OUT GARDENS

Do not formal gardens speak to us of gods, the heavens and the beginnings of the cosmos? What does the French — or as it is also called, the Classical or Baroque — garden tell us in this respect?

Space

In the seventeenth century, man's outlook on the world began to broaden. The telescope had been invented, scientists had begun to ponder over infinity and the vastness of the cosmos which had struck terror in Pascal's breast and which Europe's navigators had encountered as they roamed over the seven seas.

Over the preceding centuries, the scale of gardens had expanded, from monastic enclosures characterized by a transcendent verticality to the familiar confines of large Renaissance grounds and ultimately to the ambitious perspectives of Versailles traced by the unifying will of a Gardener-King — a king by divine right, who organized his gardens as he organized his State. It was he who decreed the axis, the center, the light.

The grounds of Versailles were landscaped to the scale of the gardens of Persepolis in order to symbolize the King's sway over his territories and subjects.

The Waterworks

The locally available water supply was insufficient, it was said. No river, no significant watercourse rans through the grounds, as if the palace had proudly chosen to turn its back on any waterway that might be used for vulgar trade or travel. But this was no obstacle. For the first time in history, a hydro-geologic study was undertaken to determine rates of flow.

Next, as early as 1616, water was brought to the thousands of waterspouts essential to the garden's splendor and the enjoyment of the King, the Court and its visitors. This was the undertaking of two Florentines, the Francine brothers. The nearest suitable water supply lay more than 24 miles away and the water had to be brought to Versailles through a system of underground conduits,

The water groves.
Opposite : the Spring Basin.
Right page : the Enceladus.

canals, pools and aqueducts ingeniously constructed to increase water pressure. There was even a plan to tap the Loire, which lay some 60 miles to the south, and to divert the river Eure through the Maintenon and Berchères aqueducts. As in the days of the pharaohs, there seemed no limit to what could be accomplished for the King's pleasure.

The original hydraulic system is still in existence. It covers more than 37000 acres and includes 100 miles of channels. It is scheduled to be restored in the years to come, and then the "Grand Musical Waters" which take place every year from Easter to All Soul's Day will truly recall Versailles' former pomp with the regularity and ampleness they displayed in their halcyon days.
The underground conduits remain unchanged since the seventeenth century and are still fed exclusively by the gravitational force of communicating vessels. The elevation of the large reservoirs in the shelter of the north wing, determines the height — almost 100 feet — of the highest water jet, the one in the Dragon Basin.
The site, let us recall, was originally marshy and had to be drained. This is one of the reasons why, as early as 1567, the Grand Canal and the Swiss Lake*, both of which regularly keep the terrain from being waterlogged, were excavated. Today, an electrical pump replaces the windmills that used to supply the force needed to move water from the Grand Canal to the upper reservoirs.

Nature Bends to Geometry

A French garden not only opens up the terrain on which it is laid out, it is also an act of will imposed on nature. In the seventeenth century there arose a spirit of experimentation informed by a triumphant and self-assured scientific knowledge, and it brought a taste for controlling nature, if not playing with it as one plays with an object hallowed by tradition that one feels henceforth entitled to manipulate. This is what happened at Versailles. Consider the vegetation tamed into perfectly-aligned walls and avenues, the right angles and uniform surfaces conquering the exuberance of branches and leaves, compelling them to the

[**Le Lac des Suisses** which gets its name from the regiment of Swiss guards that dug it between 1678 and 1682.]

9

mineral order of metal and stones. At its most extreme, this concept of landscape design leads to the topiary, the art of transforming a tree into a vase, instrument or personage.

A century later this attitude yielded to the English garden of the pre-Romantic sensibility, as far removed from Zen asceticism as from the playful seventeenth-century rationality of Versailles.
The new art of landscaping was in fact a Rabelesian cry of freedom and innocence regained. Nature, the frowning stepmother of famines and catastrophes, became a fair lady to court and flirt with.

The gardens of Versailles still move us today. When we stroll through them we experience the last tremors of the great intellectual upheaval of the Baroque era which released an irrepressible joy in humans, tinged with a new-found pride: the feeling that they could conquer their environment and were thus free.

When we stand in the middle of the Hall of Mirrors and gaze over the ample, measured and harmonious landscape of the gardens, the watery mirror of the Grand Canal and the grounds beyond it, we experience a kind of serene completeness. We gain a better understanding of the poetry of Corneille, Racine and La Fontaine; of Lully and Delalande's music; of the architecture of Mansart, Le Brun and Le Nôtre; of the sculpture of Cosyvox, Puget and Girardon. Yet our pleasure would not be so great were it not for visual breaks and surprises in the landscape. The regular central axis is beautiful, to be sure, but without the groves, the discontinuities in the perspective, the intersecting avenues, it would be merely dull.

The Groves

The term is misleading. The "groves" are not really stands of trees, but screens of vegetation and showcases. What matters is not the tree but the man-made setting, the landscape designer's imagination, his handling of symbols, his extravagance. At Versailles, each of the "groves" has its own story to tell. The underlying design of the gardens is made to form such a perfect organic whole that it leaves room for improvisation and visual entertainment.

Several groves are laid out to the south of **the central east-west axis,** with its "Tapis Vert" (**the Royal Avenue** or Great Lawn) trimmed with vases and statues.

The Ballroom or Rockery was built around 1685, featuring curtains of water sliding over rocks (brought back from Madagascar and the Red Sea) so as to blend harmoniously with the strains from the instruments of court musicians.

The Labyrinth of 1673, no longer extant but scheduled to be rebuilt in the future, repeated a traditional element in classical gardens. It was designed to house a hydraulic machine, thirty-nine fountains and statues of animals from Aesop's fables from which La Fontaine drew much of his inspiration. The animals were cast in lead and painted in natural colors. Each fable had a moral, composed by the court philosopher Benserade for the Dauphin's edification.

The Colonnade was created in 1684 by Mansart — who ventured at the King's request onto a territory where Le Nôtre was considered unrivaled. "What you have there is the work of a stonemason," the great landscape designer is said to have remarked acidly to the King. But the Colonnade is nevertheless a beautiful creation, with its arcade of polychromed marble carved by Cosyvox encircling Girardon's *Abduction of Prosperpine* (1649). It has also been christened the Music Room, and Mozart, Rameau and Couperin all performed here.
In 1815, the English-style King's Shrubbery replaced a grove called the **Royal Island.** A half-moon "mirror," or pool, is all that remains of it. After his return from the Vatican, Le Nôtre designed a **Gallery of Antiquities** — another grove that has vanished today — by positioning 24 Greco-Roman statues along a small canal that looped round a narrow, elongated island. But it was too fragile and was replaced in 1704 by the **Hall of Chestnut Trees.**

Other groves stood to the north of the Royal Avenue.
When he came to designing the **Grove of Enceladus** in 1675, Le Nôtre playfully turned to Hesiod's cosmogony for a caricature of the Fronde, the rebellion that had shaken France a quarter of a century earlier. The Titan Enceladus attempted to overthrow Zeus, who struck him down with a lightning bolt and crushed him under the rocks the rebel had piled up to reach the throne of heaven. This theme provided a wonderful pretext for a rockery, water jets, trellises and galleries more suited to lovers' trysts than political plots.
Le Nôtre was also the designer of the **Grove of Domes,** with its beautiful circular balustrade containing 44 bas-reliefs by Girardon figuring the weapons in use among the nations of the world. The balustrade disappears under sheets of water when the jets are activated.

Above: The Labyrinth of 1673
designed with animals from Aesop's fables.

Left page : The Enceladus and the Colonnade.

In 1705, the vertical thrust of the **Obelisk's** 231 jets was devised to replace the earlier Banquet Hall, an island graced by four basins and two bridges. As its name suggests, it was designed as an outdoor dining room.

Nearer to the Château stood two other groves. Both have vanished. One of them — the Three Fountains — is scheduled to be rebuilt with the help of American funds. According to one contemporary, the historiographer Piganiol, "it was the grove that owed the most to ingenuity. A great deal of art was required to turn the irregular terrain to advantage." Built on sloping ground, three fountains—the first one circular, the second one square, and the third octagonal—formed a triple flight of steps ornamented with watery arbors and cascades. Of all the groves at Versailles this was the one that celebrated the ubiquitous presence of water in the royal gardens most eloquently.

Separated from the Three Fountains by the aptly-named **Water Avenue,** or **Allée des Marmousets**, with its twenty-two groups of children designed by Le Brun, stood a grove known as the Arc de Triomphe, a tribute to Antiquity.

The vicissitudes that marked the construction of the grove known as **Apollo's Baths** remind us that it and all the other groves were chiefly designed for pleasure. In 1670, Madame de Montespan commissioned a grove called The Marsh. An extreme expression of the prevailing Baroque taste for playful combinations of exuberant forms and rare materials.
It was in these years that Mansart was charged with relocating the sculptures of Apollo Served by Nymphs, originally located in the Grotto of Tethys. The latter fountain had recently been destroyed to make room for the Château's north wing. The architect installed them on the site of the grove erected for the King's former mistress, and the fountain's name was changed to "Apollo's Baths".
In 1775, after a program of replanting the gardens was decided, the painter Hubert Robert finished landscaping the grove in the English style, with a man-made grotto, cascades and a pool.

This description of the groves and fountains in the gardens (which does not include as the Four Seasons, the Pyramid and the Nymphs) may give one the impression that the gardens as a whole lack cohesiveness. To grasp the subtlety of the gardens' overall design one must look at the global architecture of the Château grounds.

Above: the Summer Basin.

Left page: the Marmousets of the Water Avenue.

The Symbolism of the Gardens' Composition: the Two Axes

The main east-west axis organizes the gardens according to the sun's trajectory. When it rose in the east its light streamed into the King's Room and illuminated the monarch's *levée*. The setting sun was reflected on the other hand in the Grand Canal to the west. Apollo, the Olympian sun god, became a god to be honored at Versailles.

A TWO-FOLD ORIENTATION

Actually, there is an angle of 23°30

between the axis of the Grand Canal

and the point on the horizon

where the sun sets on the Summer

solstice. This divergence corres-

ponds to the angle between

the Earth equinoxial plane and the

ecliptic of the planet's course

around the sun. Hence the palace

and its grounds are organized in

relation to the celestial sun.

To the west, where the sun sets, is located the large **Basin of Apollo,** where the god's chariot is to be seen emerging from the water at dawn, pulled by four horses and surrounded by tritons and dolphins. A splendid lead sculpture by Jean-Baptiste Tuby (1668) symbolizes the rising sun setting forth on its daily journey.

In the center, the Basin of Latona recalls an episode in the life of the sun god's mother: pursued by Juno's vengefulness, Latona wanders over the earth with her two children, Apollo and Diana. Humiliated by Lycian villagers who refuse to come to her help, she asks Jupiter to change them into frogs, lizards and turtles—whose open jaws release the symphony of water jets that make this one of Versailles' finest waterworks.

To the east, but slightly off-center, stood the famous Grotto of Tethys, the sea-nymph in whose arms Apollo rested at night. Though it appears arbitrarily off-center, it too lies at an angle of 23°30 relative to true east.

This grotto was shaped like a cube with three grilles facing the palace grounds. It contained a rockery decor by Duval and mainly a hydraulic organ "controlling spurts and squirts." "At the end of the pool the organ's playing harmonizes with the song of small birds represented by shell-work in their natural state in divers recesses, and by means of an even more astonishing artifice one hears an echo repeating this sweet music."

These three works make it clear that Versailles is the palace of the sun — the sun which Louis XIV adopted as the emblem of his reign. He was not the first French monarch to do so, for the tradition of the Sun King goes back at least as far as Louis XI. But it was Louis XIV who elevated this conceit to its most meaningful and brilliant level.

The task of the artworks and the gardens which they adorn was and remains to proclaim the identity between the sun and the King. Hence the recurrent themes of time, Apollo and the wheeling planets. Time is represented by the four fountains at the garden's corners, each of which is dedicated to a different season: **Saturn** or Winter to the south and the west; **Bacchus** or Autumn to the south

Left page: the Basin of Apollo.

"*When the weary sun completes*

his task, he sinks down

toward Tethys to rest and bask.

And thus it is that Louis

goes to refresh himself."

LA FONTAINE

and the east; **Ceres** or Summer to the north and the east, and **Flora** or Spring to the north and the west. Young satyrs looking skyward surround Bacchus. Saturn gazes in the direction of the Summer solstice, while an angel searches for the position of the Winter solstice. Tipping her head backward, Ceres looks up toward the Summer solstice (the sun's zenith on June 21) next to a small angel staring eastward toward the position of the Winter solstice. Flora's eyes are directed to the position of the spring equinox and her accompanying angel, who is unusual in that he is clothed, seeks to shield himself from the sun's heat.

Thus the two male deities are located to the south; the two goddesses to the north. Symbolically, this is an odd arrangement. The portion of the year during which daylight increases, from December 21 to the 21st of June, lies to the west, and the portion of declining sunlight lies to the east. As with the symbolization of the rising and setting sun, what we have here is in fact a deliberate inversion: The west is the strong pole at Versailles, whereas all the ancient traditions stress the east, the direction from which light first appears. This is not an error that the brilliant, erudite minds of Versailles' designers, who

18

were all steeped in the love of Antiquity, were likely to have made unwittingly. On the contrary, their intention was to orient the gardens in the direction of the setting sun.

What was the reason for this re-orientation? Perhaps the natural orientation of the terrain led the King's landscape designers to open up the site toward the broad valley that lay to the west, where there was more room for expansion. The landscape converges on a vanishing point in the direction of the setting sun and gives one a sensation of infinite space. This was clearly Le Nôtre's intention. He may also have wanted to accentuate the west, for that was the direction of the voyages of discovery, especially those that revealed the Americas to the European world. Certainly there is a suggestion of progress in this orientation, in contrast to the eastward slant of tradition. One can indeed sense in this westerly bias at Versailles the assertion of a new era, one freeing itself from the hoary traditions of ancient knowledge: a robust youthfulness, unruly and proud, such as when it manifested itself in the famous dispute between the "Ancients" and the "Moderns" which left its mark, as we shall see, on the ceiling of the Hall of Mirrors.

The second axis, running north and south at a 25°30 angle from the true **north-south axis,** connects the Basin of Neptune, the Dragon Basin, the Water Avenue, the Pyramid, the aqueous "Mirrors" and the Swiss Lake. It is thus the axis of water.

To the north, the Basin of Neptune with its 99 jets and 22 vases, begun under the reign of Louis XIV and completed in that of Louis XV, marks the start of the journey along the north-south axis. For authorities on ancient myths like the artists who surrounded the King—and indeed for the King himself, tutored by the Jesuit Paulin, the libertine La Mothe, and Desmarets de St. Sorlin who taught him mythology—the north was the pole from which all life sprang, the birthplace of the first humans. At Versailles, its symbolic position is marked by a statue of Fame bearing aloft a portrait of the King! The Dragon symbolizes the power of evil, though he is also a guardian of treasures—the vanquished dragon spurting the gardens' highest jet (98 feet) amid a corolla of 17 other jets.

Detail of the Basin of Neptune.

The Basin of Neptune.

Three works come next, between two edenic groves (the Arc de Triomphe and The Three Fountains). They are followed by the **Water Avenue** with its trios of children supporting stone basins. The nature of these groups changes as you proceed south. The first is mineral, the second animal, the third becomes human with the appearance of sounds, of music. Dancing animates the fourth group and clothing distinguishes the fifth. Clearly civilization is taking hold of the figures, and with the seventh group we encounter grapes, the fruit of wine, the symbol of knowledge and superior sacrifice. In the seventh group a benevolent animal triton whose mythological parents are Neptune and Amphitrite, has replaced the grotesque marmouset of the previous groups.

This is the transition toward the Bathing Pool of Diana's Nymphs—figuring a kind of initiation rite, as any baptism must be, in the presence of the daughters of Zeus and the sky, half-sisters of the muses who invite one to strive toward joy, purity and elevated thoughts. These delightful figures naturally lead one on to the **Pyramid**, which in all spiritual traditions symbolizes knowledge and the primordial organization of the world, resting here on crayfish, dolphins and tritons — aquatic creatures all.

We now come to the North Parterre and its statuary presenting the continents, seasons, temperaments and philosophers—a veritable illustrated encyclopedia. Then a few steps more and, as if we had reached the highest platform of a temple, one now gets an unobstructed view of the entire surroundings. The Château's white stone façade projects toward the west — a huge bird extending its wings.

The design of the two wings, north and south, is based on the number 17, as is the Parthenon and, at Versailles, the façade overlooking the Marble Court. Twice seventeen windows grace each floor of the wings' façade as well as the north and south sides of the central structure. The Hall of Mirrors has a single row of seventeen windows opposite seventeen mirrors. In ancient traditions the number 17 symbolizes a passage, an intermediate stage.

Like the mirrors in the Hall of Mirrors, the two pools designed by Mansart reflect the sky. They create a link between the palace and the garden, as do the two large corner vases representing war and peace, corresponding respectively to the two reception rooms: The Salon of War to the north and the Salon of Peace to the south. Thanks to the position and the direction of their gestures, the small angels we discover here will guide us further on our journey. One of them in particular points to the Winged Children of the Sphinges, a group that seems to want to discourage us from venturing between the two Sphinges—as if Oedipus' curse had been transported from ancient Greece to this corner of the royal grounds. Actually, the two statues are guarding Apollo asleep in the Grotto of Tethys.

More richly flowered than its northern counterpart, the South Parterre overlooks the Orangerie built by Mansart in 1678, which lies further to the south and is more extensive than the one Louis le Vau designed. Both structures serve to retain the terrace of the central parterres.

The Orangerie with its superb stonework still houses some 1800 orange trees during the cold months of the year and is a splendid setting for the receptions regularly given by companies from all over the world. What is more, the gardens of the Orangerie, which will soon be rebuilt to Le Nôtre's original design, provide an excellent open space for fireworks and waterworks displays.
The Hundred Steps to either side of the Orangerie give one a precise idea of the difference in elevation between the parterres and the grounds below. They allow us to understand just how formidable an undertaking was involved in transforming an unattractive embankment into a vast, harmonious series of level spaces totally dominated by human reason.

Finally, at the southern pole of the axis, the Swiss Lake, covers an area equivalent to the Tuileries Gardens in Paris. Dug in order to provide drainage for this portion of the royal grounds, it counterbalances the Basin of Neptune to the north. Yet another mirror, its extensive tranquil surface reflects land and sky.
A large statue stands close by, oddly to one side: the equestrian statue of Louis XIV, which the French monarch commissioned Bernini to make. Finding its Roman Mannerist style excessive, the King rejected it. The rider was rechristened Marcus Curtius, a Roman hero plunging into flames on his rearing steed. The statue was banished to the very end of the southern perspective, which it dominates with its twofold suggestion of failure and bad luck.

From the terraces here another vista opens up toward the west, the privileged orientation at Versailles. In front of it stands the famous Fountain of Latona. Apollo's mother and Diana originally faced the palace, but Mansart repositioned them so that they would gaze toward the setting sun.

Left page: the Vase of War faces the Vase of Peace across the terrace in front of the Château's central building.

Below: the statue personifying the river Rhône at the corner of the Water Parterres.

A Open-Air Sculpture Gallery

A collection of statues standing on the Parterre of Latona and lining the Royal Avenue make the gardens at Versailles a splendid open-air sculpture museum. The statues along the Royal Avenue are copies of ancient Roman works executed by students at the French Academy in Rome. The Basin of Apollo at the end of the Royal Avenue is framed by a dozen statues arranged in a semi-circle.

The 2,132-foot-long Grand Canal adds a note of serenity, depth and simplicity to this ensemble. Respecting the spirit of the gardens' designer, André le Nôtre, Louis XIV resisted all attempts to close this central prospect: Mansart's suggestion that a Mount Olympus or Paranassus be raised at its western end and Puget's project of erecting a colossal statue of Apollo standing forty feet high at the intersection of the Grand Canal and its lateral extensions. In 1712, the Swedish architect Nicolas Tessin proposed building a temple of Apollo some 280 feet wide and 160 feet high, but this project too was turned down.

Opposite : the statues of the Royal Avenue.

24

THE FÊTE OF 1664

The King was mounted on one
of the finest horses in the world.
Its harness was flame-colored
and glittered with gold, silver
and precious gems. Louis XIV
was armed as an ancient Greek,
as were all the members of his
troupe, and wore a suit of silver
armor covered with a rich
embroidery of gold and diamonds.

The King later had this to say
about the celebration: "I believed
that without settling on any
one particular, less grand plan,
it should somehow represent
the duties of a prince and inspire
me eternally to fulfill them."

CARTE BANCAIRE

LE 25/04/02   09:14:46
RMN VERSAILLES
78 VERSAILLES
0107900 8999 10
509030280 101
    000113 006 000001 @ S

MONTANT = **10,98 EUR**

Pour information:
  Mont.: **72,02FRF**
  Taux : EUR=6,55957FRF

    SIGNATURE DU PORTEUR

TICKET CLIENT A CONSERVER

THE GARDENS, A SETTING FOR ROYAL ENTERTAINMENT

One reason why gardens were so much in favor with Louis XIV is that they were, for that young man skilled in the arts of seduction and manipulating symbols, an ideal terrain for maneuvers.

Interludes and Festivities

Recall that he assumed power in 1661 at the age of 23 and that it was only twenty-one years later, in 1682, that he installed his court and government at the Château. Between these two dates, the gardens were a setting for royal celebrations, illuminations, balls, banquets, theatrical and musical performances. Everything about them was perfect, grandiose, and magnificent. Royal fêtes had been a tradition long before Versailles. The kings of France had always marked their "entrance" in towns and cities with lavish festivities, like the ones that took place when 12-year-old Louis XIV and his wife entered Paris in 1650.

Nor should it be forgotten that Louis XIV was an excellent dancer. He danced on stage for the first time at the age of 13, in the ballet *Cassandra,* and he continued to perform in public until 1674. In the company of professional dancers, dancing masters and aristocrats, he performed satirical and comical roles as well as noble ones.
In France everyone from peasants to noblemen danced and *balli alle francese* were imitated throughout Europe.
Thus royal celebrations were a serious matter, if not a state affair. In his *Memoirs,* Louis XIV writes that: " Every population enjoys a spectacle, the aim of which is, at bottom, to provide pleasure; and our subjects are generally delighted to see that we enjoy what they enjoy or what they succeed in doing best. By this means we sometimes hold their minds and hearts more firmly than through rewards or benefactions."
Louis XIV's first personal decision was, in March 1661, to establish an Academy of dancing, which he entrusted to his long-time friend and ally, the Comte de Saint Aignan. It was his way of declaring that mastering the art of dancing was important to the State. Concurrently it proclaimed his wish to make dancing one of the expressions of the new monarchy's prestige and a rite of initiation at Court, so to speak.

Above: Vases from Versailles cast in lead, by Claude Ballin.

Left page: fountain "groves" delighted guests at the royal celebrations. Louis XIV gave in the gardens.

The first manifestation of this policy was the Carrousel (from *carrus sol*, the "sun's chariot"), a kind of ballet-tournament allowing aristocrats to vie with each other through the splendor of their costumes, boldness and elegance of their courtly manners.

The famous Carrousel of June 1662 at the Tuileries included five "nations", that is to say five "quadrilles" or horse troops. The Roman nation was led by the King himself, the Persian nation by the Duke of Enghien and lastly the nation «of the savages of America» by the Duke of Guise.

This was the first step of a campaign to bring France's turbulent nobility to heel, using strictly verbal weapons, a rigid etiquette— and a romantic spectacle. It was around this time that the King began to use the motto *Nec pluribus impar*, meaning "He is not unequal to many."

The celebration of the "Pleasures of the Enchanted Isles" took place in Versailles from May 7 to 13, 1664, before a chosen audience of over 500 guests (many of whom had difficulty in finding lodgings). The fête consisted of an uninterrupted succession of ballets, promenades, masked balls, banquets and spectacles. "Palaces changed into gardens, gardens changed into palaces" said La Fontaine.

Extravagantly "precious" conceits were the fashion of the day, introcued by the young Marie Mancini who had converted the 20-

year-old king, very much in love with her, to their Manneristic delights. Everyone at court was familiar with the novels that inspired these conceits, novels filled, like medieval romances, with tales of beautiful, unattainable princesses and heoes in their thrall embarking on epic adventures amid an unleashing of sentimental and meteorological tempests.

Louis XIV commissioned his chamberlain, the Count of Saint Aignan, to devise "an orderly, connected" pageant inspired by an episode from Ariosto's *Orlando Furioso,* but using settings and costumes of seventeenth-century gentlemen. The performance took place at the Rondeau des Cygnes, later to become the Basin of Apollo.
It enacted the story of a band of worthy knights being held captive in the palace of the magician Alcine. Enslaved by her beauty and appeal, they were eventually released from her charms thanks a magic ring. The Sun King, who took the role of Orlando's companion Roger, bore a shield adorned with the sun and the device *Nec cedo, nec erro!* (I neither yield nor go astray). The other knights bore shields with devices expressing their submission to the monarch. The Duke of Coislin's shield depicted a sunflower turned toward the sun, beneath the motto "His splendor stems from obedience." The Marquis de la Vallière, the brother of the King's then favorite court lady, in whose honor the pageant was held, bore a depiction of a phoenix burning in the sun's beams, with the motto, "Happiness is to be consumed by such flames."

France's haughty, fractious nobility submitted to the pageant's celestial harmony, organized with a clockwork precision that scientists like Huyghens, Cassini and Newton were soon to attribute to the laws of Creation. Perhaps it was no coincidence that the passengers of Apollo's 18-foot chariot were lords costumed as the god of the sun, the golden century, the signs of the zodiac, the seasons, and the hours of the day.

Crowning the pageant was a torch-lit banquet held in the Banquet Hall to the strains of Lully's music. The musicians played their instruments and danced in a circle round the King.The wai-

ters were costumed to look like the god Pan's servants. A few days later, the great comic playwright staged the first version in thre acts of his comedy *Tartuffe*, by special permission from the king. But almost immediatly, bowing to pressures from the queen mother, the archbishop of Perefixe and the bigoted supporters of the company of the Holy Sacrament, the monarch reversed his decision and forbade it.

On July 18, 1668, a "large entertainment" was held at the request of the King in the Château gardens, as yet in the early stages of their creation (the Basins of Apollo, Latona and the Dragon were being built and the Grand Canal was still being dug). The difference between this celebration and that of 1664 is revealing. While the gardens were the theme of the earlier fête, everything about the new celebration was designed to proclaim the majesty and power of the King, who now more than ever presented himself as an Apollo-like Sun King.
Molière staged a performance of his *Georges Dandin*, not in a theatre of greenery but in a simulated theatre adorned with statues, columns and trompe-l'oeil frescoes. Thousands of torches illuminated the Grand Canal and, capping the festivities, there was a display of fireworks that, as one contemporary writers puts it, made dawn appear at the King's command, as Felibien wrote : " It was noticed that, on that side, the night was for the most part no longer visible and the day, jealous of the advantages of such a comely night, began to show."
Gone were the earlier pageant's romantic heroes in Antique armor. The new entertainment centered on the isolated, majestic figure of the King commanding the planets to revolve at his pleasure—as they would soon to do on the painted ceilings of the vast suites in the palatial structure that Le Vau was to design shortly thereafter.

Less ambitious was the next large-scale celebration, which took place over six days between July and August 1674. It proclaimed the triumph of the Marquise de Montespan "draped in a robe of gold upon gold, re-embroidered with gold, over fleecy gold worked with a gold silk mingled with a certain gold that made it the most divine cloth ever conceived " as Madame de Sévigné describes it with subtle irony.

The King's Glory:
the Château

BUILDING THE CHÂTEAU

The 6-year-old Louis XIII, we know, discovered the unassuming, out-of-the way site of Versailles in 1607: a medieval castle on a low unprepossessing hill, remodeled in the Renaissance and belonging to the princes of Gondi.

Louis XIII's castle

To avoid having to return for the night to Paris or to his castle at Saint Germain, Louis XIII purchased 117 acres of landand had a hunting pavilion erected in 1624. This was the "picolla casa" described by the ambassador of the Republic of Venice, or, as Saint Simon put it, referring to the manor's brick-red, limestone-white and slate-blue colors the "castle of cards."

The building contained twenty-six rooms. The King's suite in the middle of the first floor included a billiard room, a royal bedchamber, a hall for granting audiences and a dressing room complete with a toilet and washing facilities. The furnishings were modest. The King's bedchamber contained a bed, two chairs, six stools and a large table standing on a leather carpet. Beside the royal apartment, there were six bedrooms for gentlemen of the royal suite, as well as quarters for a caretaker, a furniture storage room, an armory, an apothecary's cabinet and a kitchen.
Such was the seed from which the Château of Versailles grew.

Left page: the Brick Façade dating from Louis XIII.

Life in the old castle was spartan. Louis XIII would arrive toward 11 A.M. The royal chamber was chilly and the king would warm himself by standing in front of the fireplace. He would then lie down on his bed, his legs covered by his fur-lined cloak. One hour later he would arise to go and speak with his soldiers and visit his plantations in a small carriage drawn by a single horse. Next morning he would attend Mass in the church of St. Julien, return to the castle, rest, dine in his private office, go hunting and depart for Paris in the evening.

When the King came to Versailles it was alone or in the company of friends like the Count of Nogent and the Marquis of Mortemart. The only time women were invited to the castle was one day in November 1626 when Louis XIII's mother, Marie de

Medicis, and his wife, Anne of Austria, were treated to dinner before being sent away again!

In 1631, the King ordered a first series of extensions to be undertaken and little by little the Château's surface expanded to its present 200,000 square meters (over 2 million square feet).

In 1631, the King ordered a first series of extensions to be undertaken and little by little the Château's surface was to expand to its present 650,000 square feet.

This first transformation, following a design by the architect Philibert Le Roy, was completed in 1635 and cost some 250,000 livres. Meanwhile, in 1632 to be precise, Louis XIII had acquired the estate of Versailles from François de Gondi, the Archbishop of Paris. Between 1635 and 1661 the castle remained unchanged. This was the building familiar to Louis XIV up until his accession to the throne at the age of 23 and his famous dismissal of his mother, the princes, dukes and peers of France and the state ministers with the famous remark that "he would call upon them when he needed their good advice."

Louis XIV's Building Site

By 1661, Louis XIV had already earmarked 1.5 million livres for refurbishing the Château's apartments, embellishing the gardens and rebuilding the stables and servants' quarters erected in his father's reign. This was the start of his grand program at Versailles, a project that he was to unveil gradually, without ever being certain of the next step.

Versailles was not built in the manner of today's great state-inspired construction projects, with a master plan and a definite construction schedule... On the contrary, its growth was a permanent improvisation answering to developing needs and decisions arrived at during intense discussions between the Sun King, his successive chief ministers Colbert and Louvois, and his architects, landscape designers and decorators.

There is no question that the King supervised every detail of the construction from beginning to end, assisted by two successive Superintendents of Public Buildings, Colbert and Louvois. Louvois' decisions clearly expressed the monarch's desires: "The King does not wish the balustrade to be made of the stone from Tonerre, he wishes it to be of Saint-Leu stone" and "The King has ordered this be dismantled. His Majesty wants a lighter design."

In 1669 (to mention one revealing episode) the façade overlooking the Marble Court of Louis XIII's château being due for refurbishment, Colbert's chief deputy Charles Perrault declared, "we propose to tear down the small castle and in its place to erect buildings of the same nature and symmetrical design as the ones that have been recently completed"(i.e. Louis Le Vau's new stone façade on the garden side).
The King was opposed to this plan and paid no heed to Colbert's grumbling in the *Raison Générale*, the official record of the construction, that, "Anyone who has any taste for architecture...must agree that this château is like a short man having long arms and a large head, in other words a monster of a building. That is why it seems right to decide to raze it and build a large mansion instead." The King resisted, lost his patience and observed "with some feeling that if they destroyed it he would have it rebuilt as it was without a single change."
Louis XIV studied the half dozen architectural designs, which called for adding one floor to the existing building or crowning it with a dome and a steep slate roof, and rejected them all. The only change he agreed to was replacing the original five windows on each level with seven openings.

****

CHATEAU DE
VERSAILLES
GUIDERIE
*** RMN ***

25APR/2002
PUBLIC.EXT   10.98
MONTANT DU
  €URO   **10.98**

FRF   **72.02**

CB EURO
        10.98
HTAXE 5.5   10.41
TVA 5.5   .57
#001-0010   08:14R
  CAISSIER   00014

Interior plan of the Château

STATE APARTMENTS

❶ Room of Abondance

❷ Venus Room

❸ Diane Room

❹ Mars Room

❺ Mercury Room

❻ Apollo Room

❼ War Room

QUEEN'S STATE APARTMENT

❽ Peace Room

❾ Queen's Bedchamber

❿ Nobles' Room

⓫ Antechamber

⓬ Guardroom

⓭ Queen's Staircase

KING'S STATE APARTMENT

a Guardroom

b First Antechamber

c Second Antechamber

d King's Bedchamber

e Council Room

INNER APARTMENT

f New King's Bedroom

g Clock Room

h Louis XV's Bureau

i Cabinet of Dispatches

j Louis XVI's Library

k Louis XVI's Dining Room

l Billiard Room

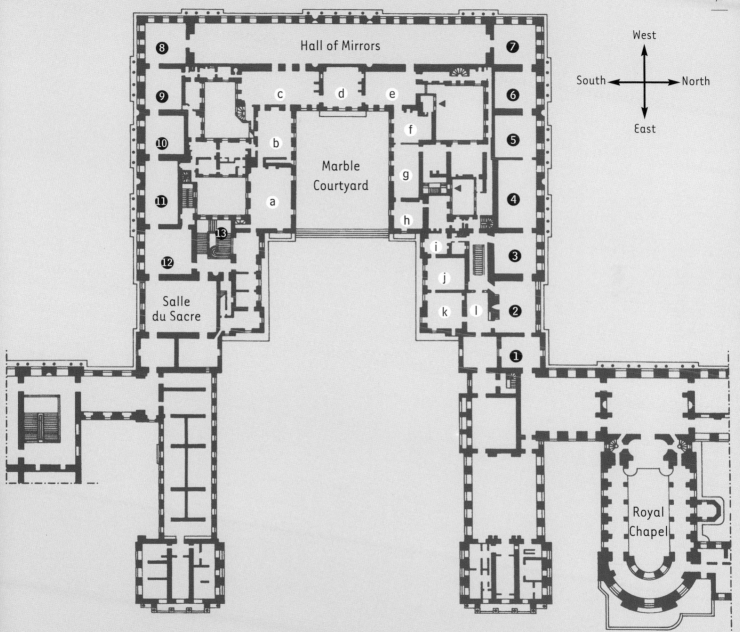

West

South ←→ North

East

Hall of Mirrors

8

7

9

6

c

d

e

5

b

f

Marble
Courtyard

10

g

4

a

h

11

3

i

13

j

12

k   l

2

Salle
du Sacre

1

Royal
Chapel

First floor of the Château

Opposite:
The Salon of Mercury was
the King's Bedchamber,
symmetrical with the
Queen's Apartments.
The decorations were
similar on both ceilings.

Right page:
The ceiling of the two
salons dedicated to
Mercury:
Mercury in his chariot
and Mercury
protector of arts.

A SYMBOLIC DECORATION

It is in the State Apartments designed by Louis Le Vau, in their original arrangement and in their decoration, every detail of which was supervised by the painter Charles Le Brun, that one can best appreciate the builder's intention to make the Château's interior a dramatic, all-embracing history lesson.

The State Apartments, a lesson in politics

To understand the organization and decoration of the State Apartments, it is necessary to know something about the Château's history.

The Hall of Mirrors, we know, did not exist in the beginning. In his 1668 design, Le Vau had conceived an Italianate loggia and terrace on the first floor between two corner pavilions. It was Mansart who, in 1680, suggested transforming the terrace into a large hall—which meant redesigning the King and Queen's apartments.

Twin royal apartments symmetrically placed at opposite ends of a central court were not an innovation at Versailles. The arrangement had already existed in royal residences since the fourteenth century. At the old castle in Saint Germain the queen's apartment was located to the south, while the king's lay to the north. Hallowed by tradition, this dual organization suggested the grouping of rooms in the State Apartments in facing pairs dedicated to a common Greco-Roman divinity.

Thus, the Hall of the King's Guards or Hall of Mars corresponded to a salon dedicated to Mars in the Queen's suite, and so too with the rooms under Mercury and Apollo's aegis. But the construction of the Hall of Mirrors shattered this symmetry and three salons on the north side of the terrace—the salons of Venus, Saturn and Jupiter—had to be redesigned.

As a result the Salon of Venus was the first state-room in the State Apartments to be reached after ascending the Staircase of the Ambassadors. The Salon of Jupiter, on the other hand, was relocated opposite the Queen's Stairs. The Salon of Saturn was simply eliminated.

Moreover, the death of Queen Marie-Thérèse in 1683, in the second year of the Court's installation at Versailles, permanently upset the balance between the two royal suites. On the birth of the Dauphin in 1729, the Queen's Bedchamber, which had originally been the Salon of Apollo in the Queen's Grand Apartment, was redecorated for Marie Leszczynska, As we see it today, this room was remodeled for Marie-Antoinette.

Another important suite, the Apartment of the King's Baths, on the north side of the ground floor, corresponded symmetrically with the seven state-rooms of the King's Apartment directly above it on the first floor. It disappeared in 1684, when its rooms were allocated to Mme de Montespan. Its present decoration dates from the 18th century, when they were occupied by the King's sisters.

The entire program for decorating the Château was decided by the Petite Académie, which got its present name of *Académie des Inscriptions and Belles-Lettres* in 1701. Set up by Colbert in 1663, this institution met twice weekly. Its members included Charles Perrault, the author of fairy tales and Colbert's chief adviser for artistic and architectural matters concerning Versailles.

The Petite Académie was a kind of ministry of culture. Its task was to choose inscriptions, mottoes, emblems and captions for monuments and medals, to oversee the writing and printing of books glorifying the King, and to administer annual gratuities to French and foreign authors. It was the Petite Académie that settled the iconographic and architectural program for the State Apartments.

The first level of reading is determined by the planets depicted on the ceiling of each state-room: they recall the attributes of a classical god

Opposite: The ceiling in the Salon of Venus.

Right page: The Salon of Diana's ceiling.

as well as the King's qualities. The royal historiographer André Félibien, the first person to describe the new apartments in 1674, explained the symbolism of the iconography: "The Sun being the King's emblem, the designers have chosen seven planets to provide the themes for the paintings in the seven rooms of this apartment. In each room are thus depicted the actions of those heroes of Antiquity associated with each of the seven planets and the actions of His Majesty." Charles Perrault, for his part, stated that "in the large paintings...are depicted the actions of the great men of Antiquity who have a connection with the planets which they accompanied and whose actions are also so exceedingly like those of His Majesty that it is possible to behold, as it were, the entire history of his reign, though no living figure is represented in them."

The goddess in the Salon of Venus is the divinity presiding over all that pertains to love. Hunting and navigating are the activities associated with Diana. Mars is the voice of war and Mercury the patron of the arts and sciences. As for Apollo, the god round whom the entire symbolic and decorative scheme centers, his territory embraces the splendor, munificence and the glory of the (then) four continents and four seasons. Jupiter's domain is justice and piety.

A second level of reading is determined by the ancient heroes present in the scenes depicted in each room. There are fifteen of them altogether and some of them figure more than once. Alexander the Great appears five times, Augustus four times, Cyrus three. Seven other Roman heroes (including Julius Caesar, the Emperors Vespasian and Trajan), four Greeks (among them Solon the Wise), as well as Nebuchadnezzar raising the Hanging Gardens of Babylon. These heroes were not intended as "role models" for the King, as would have been the case in the Renaissance, but were meant to give Louis XIV an eternal dimension. For in his own century the King embodies the virtues of each one of these heroes—and embodies them for all time: the imperial sway of Alexander, the justice of Solon, the splendor of Nebuchadnezzar, the elevated soul of Cyrus.

A third level of reading celebrates the Sun King's life in the following emblematic scenes from ancient history: Alexander the Great's wedding to Roxanna in the Salon of Venus (the room of love) is an allusion to Louis XIV's marriage ; the Carrousel of 1662 is echoed in the scene in another painting in the Salon of Venus, depicting Augustus presiding over the circus games; the War of Devolution is recalled in the depiction of Cyrus arming himself to save a princess (Salon of Venus); Alexander the Great hunting a lion in the Salon of Diana are celebrations of royal hunts; the Sun King's victories depicted in the Salon of Mars echo those of Cyrus in the war god's salon; the Salon of Mercury proclaims the king's munificence as patron of the arts.

Thus every detail in the King's State Apartment was designed, as Perrault requested, to proclaim the eternal glory of the then 30-year-old monarch. No comparable program exists for the Queen. To be sure, the Queen's Apartment includes depictions of classical heroines, but they celebrate greatness, courage and intelligence—virtues associated with the Sun King rather than with the Queen. She rates no apotheosis like Marie de Medicis' at the Louvre. The symmetry of the two State Apartments is a fiction. The palace of Versailles celebrates one, and only one, sovereign—the Sun King.

Speaking before the Petite Académie that settled the iconographic program for the State Apartements, Louis XIV declared : "Gentlemen, you can appreciate the esteem in which I hold you by the fact that I have entrusted to you the thing I hold dearest in the world—my glory."

THE HALL OF MIRRORS, A SHOWCASE FOR THE KING

The Hall represents the King's life in a new manner: the "Moderns" having triumphed over the "Ancients," the artists felt free to celebrate their own times rather than ancient scenes. The King was now boldly depicted and History was shown in the making — the equivalent of news on television.

Building the Hall

The decoration that we see today in the Hall of Mirrors, or Grand Gallery, is the result of a carefully-thought-out decision by Louis XIV assisted by the researches of the Petite Académie. Le Brun's initial project, presented in 1679, centered on the painter's favorite Apollonian theme. The program for the Hall of Mirrors included 140 figures and was to crown the "avenue of light" created by 17 mirrors reflecting the gallery's 17 windows facing the gardens.

But Louis XIV vetoed this project, perhaps because he did not wish a repetition of the theme that Le Brun's leading rival Mignard had executed masterfully at Saint-Cloud in the palace of Monsieur, the King's brother. Le Brun next proposed an allegory on the theme of the labors of Hercules, depicting "the actions of the King and the war then being waged against Germany, Spain and Holland."
This was a far more heroic subject than the theme of Apollo, and it was also a more pious one, for it shows Hercules repenting, converting and ascending to Heaven in glory. Having first appeared in the court of Burgundy in the 14th century, it was a familiar theme in the royal courts of Europe, for Hercules was said to have sired 70 children, and thus any ruler could easily claim descent from him.

This project too was rejected. Louis XIV wanted something more political. The decision to commission a new project was taken in the High Council where important matters of state, especially foreign policy matters, were decided. Colbert recorded that the

The girandoles of the Hall of Mirrors date from the reign of Louis XV.

decision was "made with the prudent restriction that it was to include nothing that was not in accordance with the truth or anything onerous to the foreign powers it might involve."

The fashion of the times was for History and no longer strictly for mythology. In 1676, Boileau and Racine were appointed historiographers of the King and ordered two years later to be present at the capture of Ghent by royal troops led by the King.

The work of decorating the gallery began in 1680 and lasted four years. Two-thirds of it was finished by the time the Court moved into Versailles in May 1682. The Salon of War and the Salon of Peace were only completed in 1686, under the supervision of Louvois, who succeeded Colbert after the latter died in 1686.

As with the Labyrinth erected around the same time, the pet project of Charles Perrault who conceived and "explicated" it, the Grand Gallery was not only meant to be appreciated for its iconographic details, it was designed to be read as an artistic whole.

By September 1683, Louvois, the newly-appointed Superintendent of Public Buildings, commissioned François Charpentier, the Permanent Secretary of the Académie Française, to compose—in French, not in Latin—a series of texts to accompany the paintings in the gallery. But Charpentier's style was deemed too pompous and his mottoes were given to Boileau and Racine to rewrite. The Grand Gallery must be considered as a political memorial to the events of the age in France and Europe, and the ideal representation of the King Louis XIV.

The Dome

The central painting in the decorative scheme was situated where the east-west and north-south axes intersect. Its inscription was "The King governs by himself." A dome, a traditional architectural structure for depictions of immortality, would normally have been conceived for this location. The painting that replaces it, depicting the young Louis XIV's accession to the royal throne— the dawn of his reign— echoes the sculpture group of Apollo driving the sun's chariot in the gardens.

In Charpentier's first version,

the inscription of the Hall

of Mirror's central painting

proclaimed "The King prefers glory

to pleasures." Charpentier then

expanded it to, "Louis the Great,

in the flowering of his youth,

took the helm of the State and,

forgoing repose and pleasure,

gave himself over entirely

to the love of true glory."

Racine and Boileau's version, which

the King preferred, stated simply,

"THE KING GOVERNS BY HIMSELF."

Starting from this central location large paintings depicting the two first wars of the King's reign—the War of Devolution and the Dutch War—articulate a labyrinthine message. The oval and octagonal paintings are connected in a zigzag reading from north (War) to south (Peace). The garden side is dedicated to diplomacy, the mirror side celebrates military victories, and the central axis emphasizes the King's attention to the physical and spiritual security of his subjects (his measures to increase security in Paris and to combat famine and duels, the campaign to take Dunkirk from the Protestants).

The four ovals surrounding the central arch represent France's restored financial order, the royal patronage of the Fine Arts, the re-establishment of navigation, and the reformed judicial system. The accent is no longer on verticality, as in churches. Rather, as in the Château gardens, the horizontal dimension predominates in the Gallery and its two connecting salons.

Salon of War and salon of Peace : a political memorial

By a secret decision of the High Council, the Hall of Mirrors was dedicated to the King's just cause in the Holland.

At the north end, the Salon of War features France at the center of the ceiling, surrounded on three sides by the hostile powers opposing Louis XIV's armies in Holland. The enraged goddess Bellona, flanked by allegories of Rebellion, Discord and the evil consequences of war, can be seen on the fourth side.

On the south end, the Salon of Peace, France again occupies the center, but this time she is depicted bringing peace to Europe through a series of royal marriages (the marriage of the Dauphin to the Elector of Bavaria's sister and that of the King of Spain and Marie-Louise of Orléans, as well through Christianity's victory over the Ottomans and the King's policy of re-establishing the arts. The Germans are shown resuming their tippling, the Spanish go back to dancing, and the Dutch are seen returning to work.

Between the salons of War and Peace, the large paintings in the Hall of Mirrors depict the cause of the Dutch War: the earlier War of Devolution for the claims of the King and Queen, who had been compelled to surrender the Franche-Comté at the Peace of Aix-la-Chapelle—an iniquitous peace concluding a just war. We next see the King, flanked by the warlike Mars and the cautious Mercury pointing out the ravages of warfare, as he ponders the decision to send troops against the Dutch. Justice tips the scales in favor of what is perceived as a just cause.

The monarch's figure

The monarch's figure as portrayed in the Hall of Mirrors is represented differently in the paintings in the Grand Apartments. The Sun King is not depicted as a classical hero, but as a real flesh-and-blood King — Louis XIV, with his wig and characteristic features and attitudes. He is the only living human being to be portrayed realistically. Or more or less realistically, for he is represented as a Roman emperor to signify the immortality of his glory. He is always shown standing above the other figures, crownless but bearing the insignia of authority — a motionless, impassive monarch capable of listening and deciding., his eyes expressing nothing but their own superiority, his features utterly inscrutable.

The Salon of War and the Salon of Peace balance each other at opposite ends of the Hall of Mirrors

LIFE AT COURT

Though he decided to "create Versailles" as early as 1663, it was not until 1682 that Louis XIV took up residence there with the Court, the royal household and his government.

An Original Political System

In 1682, Versailles became the official seat of the Court and government. The Château became a town in itself and court etiquette became increasingly formal in keeping with the spirit of the palace — a seat of royal glory and grandeur. But this was also a period of mourning: Colbert died in 1683 and, in July of the same year, so did Queen Marie-Thérèse of Austria. The following October, the King secretly married Madame de Maintenon, making her the first lady of the Château. Her fussy modesty had a certain hold over the King, especially after 1701 when he began to meet with her daily and deliberate with his ministers on State matters in his private office.

The visitor to Versailles should be aware that Louis XIV's reign falls into two distinct periods. From 1660 to 1690, a period of youth, energy and successes, the King was surrounded by able advisers who laid the foundations of France's economic, moral and military power.

After 1690 came a time of crises (the catastrophes of 1693-1649, which cost some 1.3 million lives out of a total population of 22 million), military and diplomatic setbacks (especially the War of the League of Augsburg which ended France's hegemony) and financial and commercial problems (i.e., the failure of numerous French colonial companies).

But this was also the era of the King's personal rule. Louis XIV's chief minister, Colbert, who had overseen the construction of the palace and the gardens at Versailles, had died and so had his successor, Louvois. The personal policies that the King began to implement in 1691 did not have the moral and intellectual scope of the first period. This was the start of the absolute monarchy, as it has been termed, a system of consolidated government resting wholly on the glory, skill and steadfastness of one person—the King.

By means of an original political organization designed to bring the high nobility to heel and to develop a prosperous mercantile economy, Louis XIV succeeded for some time in maintaining this equilibrium, which was later to crumble under the assaults of the French Revolution.

We must be quite clear about the meaning of the word "absolute". The Latin *absolutus* means free of all restraints, in other words responsible to God alone. Louis Dieudonné was a monarch by divine right. This explains the solemn ceremonies of the King's *levée* in the morning and his retiring at night. The King's Bedchamber was like a chapel with an altar rail dividing the faithful from the tabernacle enclosing the host (the King's bed and his divine body). Even when the King was not lying in bed, his courtiers would genuflect in front of it, as though it was an empty tabernacle.

Above : The chapel where the King attended Mass daily in the Royal Gallery and the Council Chamber. Right page: The King's bed.

A Day in the King's Life

At 7:30 a.m., a valet, who had spent the night in the royal bedroom, would wake up the King and summon the First Physician and the First Surgeon to examine the monarch.

At 8:15, the King's current First Gentleman-in-Waiting (there were four such officers, each one serving for one year out of four) opened the curtains of the royal bed and ushered in the royal family, the royal princes and the high officials of the Royal House. A 15-minute service was then held in the presence of the chaplain on duty. Every other day, the King was shaved by his personal barber and the Gentleman-in-Waiting then presented the monarch with the first of the three wigs he would wear in the course of the day. The King then rose from his bed to receive the second *entrée*, consisting of Court officials (his four cabinet secretaries, the First Valets of the Wardrobe, the Intendant and the Comptroller of the Royal Silverware) and courtiers who had a *brevet d'affaires* entitling them to pay their respect to the monarch seated on his *chaise d'affaire*, i.e. his privy (the 17th century notion of shame being very different from ours). The King then breakfasted, watched by titled visitors, where upon he dressed and knelt for the second prayers of the day.

At 10 o'clock the King crossed the State Apartment to attend Mass in the chapel (an obligation for the whole Court). Subjects wanting to draw his attention to a particular claim would station themselves along the way. After Mass, the King would retire to the private office next to his bedroom and devote some time to his "King's trade." It was here that his principal council meetings took place: the High or State Councils (on Sundays, Mondays and Wednesdays) which included 3-7 members, the cabinet meetings of the State ministers, the councils of the Royal Finances (on Tuesdays and Saturdays) and the *Conseil des Dépêches* devoted to the reports of the King's ambassadors, governors and intendants. On Thursdays the King gave private audiences, notably to the architects and gardeners employed at Versailles. On Fridays he saw

his confessor and made ecclesiastical nominations. When the King required a break from his duties, musicians or writers were summoned to his office.

At one o'clock there was a Petit Setting (i.e.; a light lunch) for the King in his room with the members of the royal family who, at best, sat on stools at some distance from the monarch, and courtiers who were obliged to stand. The ceremony of the King's luncheons were rigid and ponderous, requiring at least twenty persons in attendance. The "Bouches du Roi" meal services could mobilize as many as 500 people. The King would then change and stroll through the gardens, often down to the Grand Canal where a flotilla of pleasure boats awaited him. The King would install himself in a gondola, surrounded by a few ladies of the Court and accompanied by musicians and singers.

Some time between 4 and 5 o'clock, the King would return to his apartment, change into his finest clothes, write a few "friendly missives", visit Madame de Maintenon in her apartment, and, three days a week (Monday, Wednesday and Thursday) he would attend evenings in the Grand Gallery salons.
Buffets were offered in the salons of Diana and Venus, the King and his courtiers played billiards—a game he was especially fond of—,there was dancing and musical performances in the Salon of Mars, and everywhere there was card-playing. Accompanied by two *gardes de la manche*, the King strolled around, spoke a few words here and there, greeted courtiers and listened to his musicians (the King's Music included singers and instrumentalists who performed during chapel services and during dinners in Mme de Maintenon's apartment).

At 10 o'clock the King sat down in public for a light meal accompanied by music in the Queen's Antechamber. Around 11 o'clock he went to his office, where he spent some time with his family.
A grand and petit nighttime ceremony would then take place similar to the morning's *levée*, but in reverse order. It ended with the King giving a password to the commanding officer of his personal security guard, while Swiss guards settled down for the night on folding beds in the Hall of Mirrors.

Above: 17th century costumes.

Right page: Louis XIV received courtiers in the Château's former chapel, by A. Pezey (1695-1710).

56

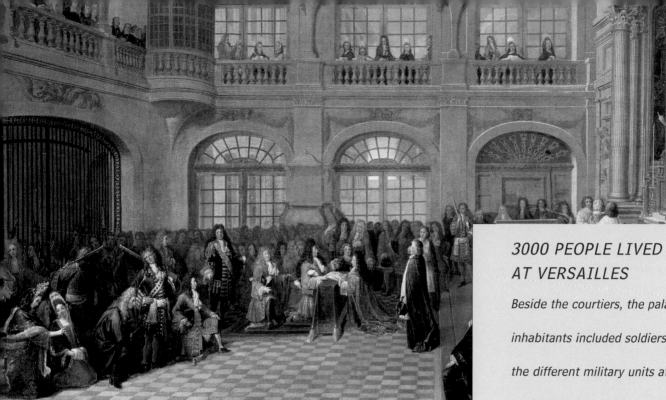

The Court

In comparison to this meticulously-programmed royal life on permanent public display, the life of the courtiers was fairly uncertain. To begin with, how many courtiers were present at Versailles? The Court consisted of the member of the royal family, the royal princes, ecclesiastical princes, some thirty dukes and royal peers, and roughly a hundred high State dignitaries. All were entitled to reside in the palace. Then came all the other members of the nobility who were drawn to Versailles by the presence of the King and his favorites and the prospect of obtaining a pension and other benefits for themselves, their family, relatives and clients.

Versailles was, in a sense, Louis XIV's instrument for bringing France's proud, independent, contentious nobility under his yoke. To be sure, there were never more than 4,000 or 5,000 nobles residing at the palace, out of an aristocracy that numbered some 200,000 members. But the country's leading aristocrats, those whose connections spread to every corner of France, were present at Versailles.

3000 PEOPLE LIVED AT VERSAILLES

Beside the courtiers, the palace's inhabitants included soldiers from the different military units attached to the Royal House, the French and Swiss guards—a total of nearly 10,000 men but, with the exception of the King's personal security guards and the "100" Swiss guards, they were not actually garrisoned at the Château. The palace servants, musicians and artists included a further 4000 persons. The number of courtiers to whom Louis XIV, skillfully and cynically doling out promotions and demotions, assigned quarters in the palace is reckoned to be about 3,000.

TRADING FAVORS

The royal house is like a vast

market to which it is necessary

to go in order to trade for

our livelihood and for the interests

of those to whom we are bound

by duty or friendship.

MADAME DE MOTTEVILLE

By this means Louis XIV managed to govern the country with a very small number of civil servants, as we would call them today. He was able to compromise with the country's oligarchies, giving them a free rein in all matters with the exception of diplomacy, war, taxes and public works. Moreover, the court nobility set the fashion in Paris and the provinces, which helped to unify the French nation.

Being in Court was like managing a nest egg. The principal aim of every courtier was to approach the King and ask him to grant a favor. This meant spending hours every day in places where the King was expected to walk past, in the hope of attracting his attention. And this in turn involved upholding one's rank and sparing no expense—not an easy task for lords who derived their income from distant, often badly-farmed estates run by stewards who took their own share of the profits. Thus many courtiers lived from hand to mouth, running up debts and trading favors. A well informed courtier who passed on news about a new government bureau being set up could expect to receive a "liberality" in return.

Toward the end of Louis XIV's reign, the influence of Madame de Maintenon's austere and pious views and the weariness of a monarch worn out by ill-health and the death of members of his royal circle increased the atmosphere of boredom that had always pervaded the highly artificial life at Court.

Many of the King's courtiers were dead or very elderly. The Court waited with a certain impatience for the aging monarch to breathe his last and plotted with his nephew, the Duke of Orleans, who would become the Regent.

At 8:15 in the morning on September 1, 1715, Louis Dieudonné passed away. Without even waiting for his body to be transported to the royal basilica of Saint-Denis, many of the courtiers packed up and left Versailles.

Left page: Louis XIV equetrian statue.

After Louis XIV :
New Customs in the Age of Enlightenment

LOUIS XV : THE INVENTION OF PRIVATE LIFE

Though the Château was built by Louis XIV, Louis XV was the king who resided the longest at Versailles. He settled there in 1722 and died in 1774 at the age of 64, the second and last monarch to breathe his last in the palace.

A More Refined Château

Louis XIV died on September 1, 1715. A little more than a week later, on September 9, the Regent left Versailles, taking the young Louis XV with him to Vincennes. The Court scattered and the administration returned to Paris. The Duke of Noailles proposed tearing down the palace. But in June 1722, one month before the 12-year-old Louis XV reached the age when he could be proclaimed King, Cardinal Dubois brought the future monarch back to Versailles. The boy romped through the palace and gardens for several hours before going to pray in the chapel and lying down on the parquet floor of the Hall of Mirrors to admire Le Brun's ceiling paintings. He was crowned at Rheims on October 22 of that same year.

The new King was intelligent and filled with curiosity, but he was shy and melancholy by nature, prone to boredom and macabre thoughts. He disliked crowds and although he lent his presence to court ceremonies he was at ease only in small, private apartments. In his daily life, he no longer clung to Louis XIV's rigid timetable. He enjoyed spending his evenings with a few friends in the refined setting of his second-floor apartments.

Left page : Music Room of Louis XV's daughter, Madame Adélaïde.

61

MIGNARD'S PETITE GALLERY UNDER LOUIS XIV

In 1685, Le Brun's chief rival, the painter Pierre Mignard, decorated a small gallery and two salons dedicated to the arts and sciences. Here, in Madame de Montespan's former suite, he depicted Prometheus stealing fire from heaven and Vulcan fashioning Pandora from earth. The walls were lined with mirrors, tortoise-shell decorations, consoles and capitals for displaying royal gems and jewelry.

First, he rendered etiquette less stiff and formal. There were two aspects to his daily life as King: his public appearances in the State Apartments of Louis XIV and his private life in Louis XIII's original dwelling at Versailles, the interior of which he remodeled and redecorated to his own taste. Louis XV wanted a more intimate setting and in 1735 he commissioned Gabriel, Rousseau and Verberckt to design a handsome decorative ensemble in the right wing overlooking the Marble Court.

The room that lay closest to the Council Chamber became the King's Bedchamber in 1735. It contained a canopy bed, two armchairs, a cabinet, and had a water closet with running water and a toilet.

Next came a Clock Room embellished with a magnificent astronomic timepiece designed by Claude-Siméon Passemant that depicted the movement of the planets, the phases of the moon, the month, day of the week and hour, with a truly stunning precision for a clock made to keep time until the year 9999 ! The meridien of Versailles is represented on the floor — yet another indication of the King's interest in the scientific knowledge of his time.

Then came, beside the Dog's Room of his ancestor, an innovation at Versailles (in 1735): a private dining room where the King received a few select friends and his reigning mistress. Louis XV's penchant for private life led him to create a special dining room for meals among family or a few select friends — an innovation that would quickly spread to the town houses of the aristocracy and the upper middle class.

Louis XV's Bureau was located across from the Clock Room. This too was an innovation, for the royal apartment had previously never included such an office, however essential it seems to the running of the State. The finest item of furniture in this room was — and remains — a rolltop desk designed by the cabinetmaker Riesner, in whose drawers the King kept his secret papers. Thanks to an ingenious mechanism all of the desk's drawers could be opened by a single key permanently in the King's possession.

Above: Passemant timepiece.
Right page: the rolltop desk in the Bureau of the King.

Marie Leszczynska's Cabinet in the Queen's Petit Apartment.

The King, who had been compelled to have his daughters—with the exception of Adelaïde, the youngest—educated at the Abbey of Fontevrault, turned over the nearest of his office suites to this last-born princess. One room in this suite can still be visited today, with its remarkable carved wainscoting depicting musical instruments—for it was in fact designed to be the music room.

An intelligent monarch who was nicknamed the "Well-Loved", Louis XV was also a sceptic suspicious of everyone and everything. A secretive man, he set up an official secret service known as the *Secret du Roi*. Running this network required having a room where the King could receive envoys discretely, a special room that had several separate entrances. It was named the **Cabinet of Dispatches** and though the diplomacy conducted within its walls was not especially successful, this bureau located next to the King's private office is a particularly fine addition to the Château and has recently been restored.

Life at Court

Life at Court reflected this more personal approach. Henceforth, it was duty, not favor currying, that brought the nobility to Versailles. Only courtiers having an official capacity were authorized to live at the Château—and only when on official duty. Many of them had their own residence in the town of Versailles or in Paris.

Louis XV, like his great-grandfather Louis XIV, enjoyed the company of women and was a master at leading a double life. He was 15 when he married 22-year-old Marie Leszczynska, who gave birth to ten children in just a dozen years. Marie Leszczynska slept in the Queen's Bedchamber in the southern State Apartment. It was here that the royal couple's eight daughters and two sons were born. Fabre and Verberckt refurbished the room's decoration with gilded wainscoting and a ceiling painting by Boucher. The inner cabinets were remodeled to provide the Queen with more comfortable quarters for dining and giving audiences. A "laboratory" was even designed for her, where she did tapestry work, painted under Andresy's guidance and occasionally meditated in candlelight.

A NEW VERSION OF THE KING'S LEVEE

"When I get up before my servants enter the room, I light my own fire and have no need to summon anyone <...>. Those poor fellows need their sleep, I deprive them of rest quite enough as is."

LOUIS XV

65

The Queen filled her role as a sovereign with discernment and dignity. She died as she had lived — discretely — on June 24, 1768.

Louis XV had a number of official mistresses, including the three sisters of the Marquis of Nesles and especially Jeanne Antoinette le Normand d'Etioles, née Poisson, a commoner he met at the masked ball given on February 25, 1745. In the summer of 1745, the King made her the Duchess of Pompadour and two months later he installed her in the palace. In spite of the secret plotting of her enemies, Madame de Pompadour's reign at the King's side lasted two decades. For she entertained the King and distracted him from his spells of existential ennui. She briefly inspired a vogue for theatrical performances in the Staircase of the Ambassadors, acted out by members of leading aristocratic families. She was Louis XV's confidante, his closest adviser on all matters including political and diplomatic ones. From 1753 to her death at 41 in 1764, she was the friend with whom he shared his sorrows and troubles. She was granted the exceptional privilege of being allowed to die in the palace.

After the Queen's death, the King fell in love with another commoner, the beautiful Jeanne Becu, who succeeded through an intrigue in marrying the Comte du Barry in 1768. The King settled her in the palace a few months later, despite the Duke of Choiseul's remark, "We did not think that such a low intrigue could have had any other consequences than those of a passing fancy."
When Marie-Antoinette arrived in the French Court after her marriage to the Dauphin in 1770, she allied herself with the King's daughters in a struggle against Madame du Barry, ignoring the advice of her mother, the Empress Maria Teresa of Austria: "You must not think of, or look upon, la Barry in any other way than as a lady admitted to Court and to the King's society; you are his first subject."
After the King's death, Marie-Antoinette took revenge on Madame du Barry by having her locked up in a convent.

To be entitled to the "honors of the Court", one had to belong to an aristocratic family going back to at least 1400 and to have been sponsored and introduced to the King and Queen by a member of

Court. This entitled one to certain privileges, such as being invited to royal celebrations, receptions and gaming circles and having the right to ride in one of the King's Coaches. The return to ancestral prerogatives inevitably fostered cliques, clans and intrigues at Court and contributed to an increasingly unruly attitude among the nobility and to a general decline in respect for the King. The aristocracy began to see itself as a separate "country" within the country, stressing by its behavior its distinctness from the bourgeoisie, inventing a virtual language of its own, with its special vocabulary, locutions and pronunciation (for example dropping the final *c* in such words as *sac* and *tabac*). This kind of thing did not make Madame de Pompadour's life any easier. Hardly thirty years had passed since the death of Louis XIV, yet his reign seemed already very much a thing of the past. A courtier had no option but to take sides. He had to belong to Madame de Pompadour's camp, to that of her arch-enemy Maurepas or to the Duke de Choiseul's clan.

LAMPOON AGAINST MME DE POMPADOUR

"Graced with neither wit nor character, but having an avid, empty soul, La Pompadour gossips like a fishwife — and no wonder, she's a Poisson (i.e. a fish)! Such a foolish creature is she, low in every respect and flat of face, that everyone deems the King quite mad to make her the talk of the Court."

This did not prevent increasingly splendid festivities and celebrations from being held at Court, with tens of thousands of spectators gawking at ever more elaborate firework displays.

The Fireworks of 1729 in honor of the Dauphin's birth was held in the Chateau's forecourt and when it ended, a contemporary chronicler reportes, "the paved road from Versailles to Paris was an unbroken succession of carriages." Another fireworks display was organized in August 1739 for the wedding of Louis XIV's eldest daughter and the Spanish Infante. It was ignited on the Tapis Vert (Great Lawn) at the signal of a rocket fired from the Hall of Mirrors by the King himself.

For the wedding festivities of the Dauphin Louis-Auguste—the future Louis XVI— and Marie-Antoinette of Lorraine and Austria, on May 16 1770, Louis XV commissioned the architect Jacques-Ange Gabriel to design a building that would serve as an opera, ballroom and State banquet hall. The architect put to work the artisans of the "Menus Plaisirs" (the King's Entertainment), who were sklled in working rapidly in wood to create a wide variety of decors and mechanical devices. Louis XV thus made one of his ancestor's dreams come true: he built a permanant theater at Versailles.

The Royal Opera was thus erected entirely in wood. Its acoustics were exceptionally good, thanks to a skilful adaptation of the ancient Greek technique of placing amphorae under stairs to capture echoes: wooden columns were used to achieve the same result. The theater was equipped with a wealth of machinery, trapdoors and hoists. The stage could be lower to create a single spacious area for balls and royal banquets. To make the illusion complete, the bal paré decor behind the stage repeated the decoration of the opera hall, extending its sides to form a perfect oval.

It was here that the wedding banquet took place. 24 musicians performed for the very select 22 guests who sat at the royal table and their guests who dined in the boxes tiered above them.

The next day, Lully and Philippe Quinault's opera *Perseus* was performed amid general boredom. This was followed, on the third day, by the Gala Ball marred by a mix-up in protocol which was

The Royal Opera designed by Jacques-Ange Gabriel.
For acoustical reasons, it was entirely constructed
with imitation-marble wood panels.

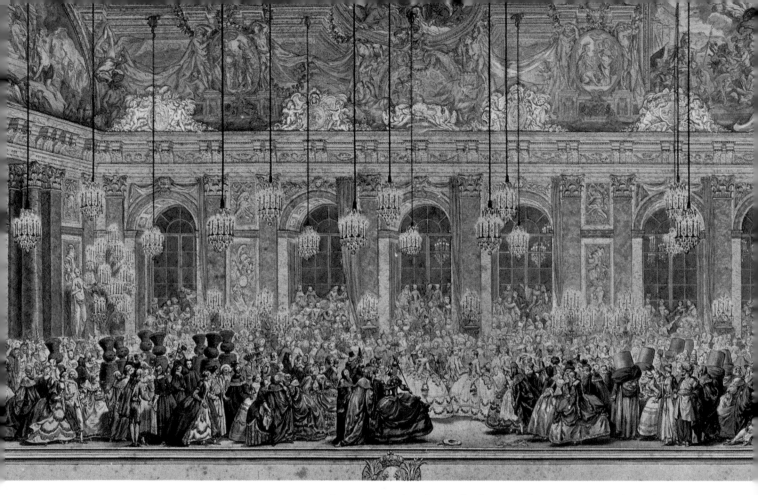

The masked ball given for the wedding of the Dauphin—the future Louis XVI — where Louis XV appeared dressed as a yew tree. By Nicolas C. Cochin (1715-1790).

taken very seriously — the house of Lorraine preceding the royal duchesses in the order of the dances — while orchestras played in the gardens and a magnificence fireworks display dazzled the tens of thousands of spectators who had converged on Versailles from the four corners of Europe.

Cascades, pyramids and whirling suns emblazoned with the coat of arms of France lit up the night sky. 20,000 gold and silver rockets burst above the trees in a final salvo, whereupon a Temple of the Sun appeared at the farther end of the Grand Canal, while thousands of torches lit up its banks, the Royal Avenue and the palace. Then darkness descended again over the park and the French monarchy.

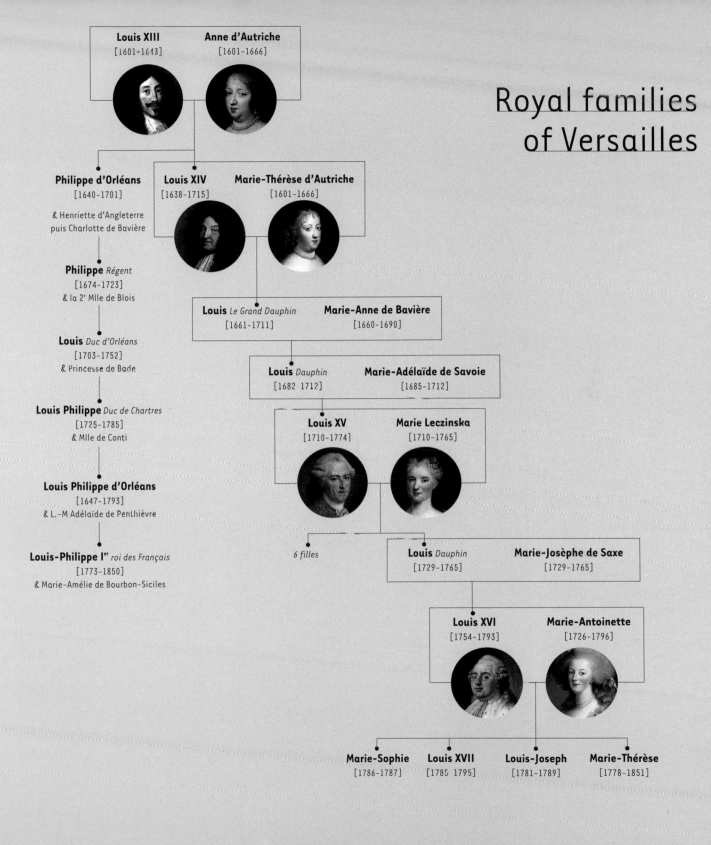

Royal families of Versailles

Louis XIII
[1601-1643]

Anne d'Autriche
[1601-1666]

Philippe d'Orléans
[1640-1701]

& Henriette d'Angleterre
puis Charlotte de Bavière

Louis XIV
[1638-1715]

Marie-Thérèse d'Autriche
[1601-1666]

Philippe *Régent*
[1674-1723]
& la 2ᵉ Mlle de Blois

Louis *Duc d'Orléans*
[1703-1752]
& Princesse de Bade

Louis *Le Grand Dauphin*
[1661-1711]

Marie-Anne de Bavière
[1660-1690]

Louis Philippe *Duc de Chartres*
[1725-1785]
& Mlle de Conti

Louis *Dauphin*
[1682-1712]

Marie-Adélaïde de Savoie
[1685-1712]

Louis XV
[1710-1774]

Marie Leczinska
[1710-1765]

Louis Philippe d'Orléans
[1647-1793]
& L.-M Adélaïde de Penthièvre

6 filles

Louis *Dauphin*
[1729-1765]

Marie-Josèphe de Saxe
[1729-1765]

Louis-Philippe Iᵉʳ *roi des Français*
[1773-1850]
& Marie-Amélie de Bourbon-Siciles

Louis XVI
[1754-1793]

Marie-Antoinette
[1726-1796]

Marie-Sophie
[1786-1787]

Louis XVII
[1785-1795]

Louis-Joseph
[1781-1789]

Marie-Thérèse
[1778-1851]

Louis XVI's Library,
the last creation
of J.-A. Gabriel.
With its trompe-l'œil
shelves painted on
the doors, it was
a haven where the King
could withdraw
in total privacy.

LOUIS XVI AND MARIE-ANTOINETTE

On their accession to the throne, the royal couple raised many hopes. The King was 20 years old, handsome, popular, generous and sensitive. The Queen was 19, striking-looking, and had a strong personality. Everyone looked to them to usher in sweeping reforms in the nation.

A Cabinet King

Louis XVI had Mme Adelaïde's suite remodelled, except for the Music Room. More even than his grandfather Louis XV, who died in 1774, he sought out the intimacy of chosen friends and the solitude of his dabbling in science. He had a series of laboratory-like cabinets built on the second floor of the palace where, a true follower of the Enlightenment, he indulged in his passion for chemistry, clock-making, physics and mechanics. He took a keen interest in the continents beyond the sea, dispatching Bougainvilliers and Lapérouse to circumnavigate the globe.

His penchant for secrecy and solitude was reflected in his **personnal library,** a retreat pervaded by the atmosphere of neatly shelved books. There, behind curtains and screens decorated in fashionable Chinese patterns, he felt free to be himself: a timid man, painstaking and punctilious. The Queen quipped cruelly, "I have married a Vulcan, but have no wish to be his Venus."

Next to the library, the room where Louis XIV formerly displayed the creations of the royal manufactories in order to promote them was turned into a simple, elegant dining room where a score of guests would dine in the company of the King and, at times, Marie-Antoinette.

Dinner was followed by games, principally billiards, the Court's chief leisure pastime since the days of Louis XIV, backgammon and cards, which were played to high stakes, particularly at Marie-Antoinette's table.

From Versailles to the Trianon : a New Lifestyle at Court

Marie-Antoinette was determined to establish her independence. Her clear-cut tastes contrasted sharply with the meekness of earlier queens. Introduced to the ceremony of "curtsies of mourning," she exclaimed before the assembled ladies of the Court dressed in black, "They're a lot of stuffed shirts, their minds belong to the last century. It would be better if all those bundles were packed off." Which earned her this gibing song: "Little twenty-year-old queen so very unwelcoming, see if we don't send you back to where you come from."

Marie-Antoinette did away with much Court etiquette, changed the ceremony of the royal levée, surrounded herself with servants she could trust and spent money lavishly at card games, on clothes and jewels. Her penchant for luxury got her unwittingly involved in the notorious affair of the Queen's Necklace, a scandal that seriously undermined the prestige of the monarchy. Worse, she allowed herself to become the prisoner of a coterie that took unlimited advantage of her and isolated her at Court.

The King was incapable of saying no to the Queen. She moved her quarters to the Petit Trianon (where she enjoyed performing in plays in her private theater) and then to the Hameau. Louis XVI struggled to keep up a minimum of protocol at Court and obliged Marie-Antoinette to return to the palace for official ceremonies. But the nobility began deserting Versailles and the Château became almost an empty shell.

One of the King's ministers, the Prince of Montbarey, later noted that "the Queen's youth and pleasure-loving ways made her view the rules of etiquette as bothersome restrictions and the people to whom they mattered as ridiculous creatures. This sovereign, who incidentally possessed rare qualities and merely had the defects of youth, paid no heed to the very useful observation that at Court appearances make more of an impression than reality. The disruption of the inner workings of the Court led to a casualness in relationships that degenerated into familiarity and, confusing everything by abolishing distance, destroyed the respect and veneration that Louis XIV, in his knowledge of the nation's character, had felt it necessary to surround himself with." The whole history of Louis XVI's unfortunate reign is summed up in these lines.

Following foreign minister Vergenne's signature of a treaty guaranteeing French diplomatic and military support to the American revolutionaries, Benjamin Franklin, the envoy extraordinary of the thirteen original states of America, was received by the King on March 2, 1778. This was the beginning of the long-standing, at times chaotic, but solid friendship between the United States and France.

May 4, 1789, saw the last "performance" of the Ancien Régime: the opening of the Estates General in the Room of the King's Entertainment, following a solemn procession from the church of Notre Dame to the church of Saint Louis. The rest is history. At 1.30 on the afternoon of October 6 a cheering revolutionary crowd conducted the King to Paris.

IDLE SERVANTS

The generally lax atmosphere at Court meant more tasks for the palace servants, all too often idle (for example, there were valets whose task was simply to announce each morning the time when the King would attend Mass) or engaged in such black market practices as selling small favors, ceremonial costumes and candles.

Louis XVI's Dining Room where items of Sèvres porcelain were displayed once a year at Christmas.

Overleaf: Marie-Antoinette's Bath-Room with its daybed.

VERSAILLES YESTERDAY AND TODAY

Impervious to human folly and fury, Versailles still offers itself to our contemplation and pleasure, as if the extraordinary craving, ambition and love of glory that gave birth to the Château and the gardens were still present.
Like the Acropolis and the Pyramids, Versailles is one of a few universal monuments that bear witness to a profound transformation of the human mind.

Before Versailles — in the Middle Ages, the Renaissance, the Baroque age — the world was an enchanted place. All forms, whether they were allegories, symbols, numbers or artworks, mirrored each other and gave a meaning to the world. As Michel Foucault observes, "Until the end of the sixteenth century, resemblance played the role of a builder in the learning of Western culture."
That civilization reached its supreme expression — and spent itself-at Versailles in the more or less openly-confessed secrets of the groves, statues and proportions that rhythm its architecture and landscape. It survives as a distant brilliance and fascinates us still today like a trace of something that has come down to us from time immemorial.

Then, too, the Château and the gardens were and still are a tremendous human challenge to Nature and to God. It was at Versailles that progress, science and rational thought, which are the foundation of our modernity, were knighted.
Everything about the Château and its setting testify to this Promethean act: the calculations of the engineers of men of science who created it; the titanic terracing and hydraulic projects; the triumphant perspectives and the feverish drive to accomplish an immense undertaking in as short a time as possible.

Two aspects of Versailles — its refining and glorifying of past traditions and its projection of the dreams and aspirations of the generations born in the Age of Enlightenment—are the key to the mystery and secret power which it possesses in common with all things that reach their apogee.

Seriors editor: Evelyne Demey

Art directors: Muriel Kerba, Caroline Renouf
Copy chief: Kellie Bourque
Grafic design: Guillaume Eschapasse
Illustration: Grimage
Engraving: GCS
Printing: SYL

Bibliography

- J. Levron, *La Vie quotidienne à la Cour de Versailles*, France-Loisirs, 1991 ;
- V. Beurtheret, *Versailles, des Jardins vers ailleurs*, A. M. D. G. édition, 1996 ;
- B. Saule, *Versailles triomphant*, Flammarion, 1996.
- C. Petitfils, *Louis XIV*, éd. Perrin, 1997 ;
- G. Sabatier, *Versailles ou la figure du Roy*, Albin Michel Histoire, 1999 ;
- P. Beaussant, *Louis XIV artiste*, éd. Payot, 1999 ;
- S. Hoog, *Jardins à Versailles*, Art Lys, 1999 ;
- C. Constans, *Versailles, Château de la France et orgueil des Rois*, Découverte Gallimard, RMN.

Photographs by:

Nicolas Bruant

Alexis Riboud : p. 14; 15; 16; 19; 20-21.

RMN :

p. 28 (G.Blot) ; p. 29 (Arnaudet) ; p. 30-31 ; p. 41 (M. Bellot ; G.Blot) ;
p. 45 ; 49 ; p. 56 (H. Lewandowski, G. Blot) ; p. 57 (G. Blot) ;
p. 70 (H. Lewandowski).